IMAGES OF ENGLAND

Canterbury

BIRTHPLACE OF MARLOWE
AT
CANTERBURY

The rear of 57 St George's Street from St George's Lane at the turn of the twentieth century. This delightful sixteenth-century house was the birthplace of playwright Christopher Marlowe. It was utterly destroyed in the Blitz of Canterbury.

IMAGES OF ENGLAND

Canterbury

Paul Crampton

NONSUCH

First published 1997
This new pocket edition 2006
Images unchanged from first edition

Nonsuch Publishing Limited
The Mill, Brimscombe Port,
Stroud, Gloucestershire, GL5 2QG
www.nonsuch-publishing.com

Nonsuch Publishing is an imprint of Tempus Publishing Group

British Library Cataloguing in Publication Data.
A catalogue record for this book is available from the British Library.

ISBN 1-84588-257-1

Typesetting and origination by Nonsuch Publishing Limited
Printed in Great Britain by Oaklands Book Services Limited

Contents

Acknowledgements

I would like to thank the following for supplying photographic material, namely Anthony Swaine, Neil Mattingley, Stan Kemp, Derek Butler, Gerry Whittaker, Ted Yeoman, Malcolm Harvey, David Cowley, Paul Tritton and Kate Urry.

Furthermore, a special vote of thanks must go to the photographers whose work appears herein, namely Patrick Brown, Ben May, Barrie Stretch, Edward Wilmot, David Cousins and the late Mr W. Fisk-Moore.

My final words of appreciation must go to those who allowed me to use material from their archives, namely *The Kentish Gazette*, Canterbury Museums, Robert Brett & Sons Ltd and English Heritage (RCHM).

I am always on the lookout for further photographic material of Canterbury from any era. This includes the more unusual postcard views. If you have such material and are prepared to make it available, I would be pleased to hear from you. Please write to me at 11 Little Meadow, Upper Harbledown, Canterbury, Kent CT2 9BD. Many thanks.

Introduction

Welcome to this pictorial journey through the streets of Canterbury, one of the most well known and best loved cities in Britain. Photographs from the 1880s to the 1980s are included, many showing startling changes that have occurred over the years. These pictures have been extensively cross-referenced to allow the reader to compare views of the same location in different periods.

I have striven to include a large amount of rare and previously unpublished photographs, as well as a few more familiar ones. Moreover, lesser-known back streets and lost buildings enjoy equal representation with our main thoroughfares and more familiar landmarks.

Our leisurely saunter through the lanes and streets of the city takes place in six different periods, each represented by its own chapter. Not only are many lost scenes and buildings included, but also the vehicles and people of each era are very much in evidence.

In Chapter One, we see Canterbury as it was before the Blitz, in many respects a city little changed from the early post-mediaeval years. However, it is wrong to assume that modernisation only occurred after the Blitz. Indeed, this process was already well underway in the 1930s. Between the wars, many hundreds of ancient terraced houses within the city walls were demolished under various slum clearance schemes. At the same time, new council house estates appeared on former farmland on the outskirts of the city. Along the main street, new shops were replacing old ones and a new hospital emerged that put its predecessor to shame. The years following the Great War also saw a number of our key historic buildings being saved from dereliction and/or demolition, including the Blackfriars and Castle Keep. Pictures of both are included in this book.

Photographs in Chapter Two graphically illustrate the devastation wrought by the 1942 Blitz on the south-east quadrant of the city. Also shown are damaged buildings that fell victim to the all too thorough clearance operation afterwards. The Cathedral's lucky escape from serious damage is also shown in this chapter.

During the late 1940s plans for the rebuilding of the flattened parts of the city were formulated. However, this process was not without its difficulties. The 1945 Holden Plan that proposed the comprehensive redevelopment of the whole city had effectively been voted out in the local elections of November of that year. Its replacement, largely formulated by City Architect Hugh Wilson, was a far less radical plan and, with a little arm twisting, it was approved by both council and electorate.

Nevertheless, there were still problems, including what to do with the remains of St George's Church, many pictures of which are included in Chapter Three.

The rebuilding of Canterbury began in the early 1950s and is extensively covered in Chapter Four. The traditional and somewhat conservative new buildings of the Dean and Chapter provide an interesting contrast with the modern, mostly flat-roofed, yet carefully planned, buildings put up by the City Council. Elsewhere in Canterbury, local firms expanded or modernised their premises, especially those concerned with the motor vehicle trade.

At this time, there was a genuine civic pride in the achievements of the planners and in those new buildings that emerged under the auspices of the Wilson Plan, as well as those built under private enterprise. This was demonstrated by the fact that famous celebrities and members of the government were regularly invited to attend opening ceremonies. A number of these distinguished visits are recorded in Chapter Four.

In Chapter Five, we look at the 1960s, an era of extensive demolition. Modern shops began to spill into parts of the city largely untouched by the Blitz. Furthermore, ideas first formulated in the 1930s were finally put into practice, not least of which was the construction of a ring road. The slum clearance programme, suspended in the early 1940s because of the Blitz and the resultant housing shortage, was restarted in earnest. Sadly, slum clearance was sometimes used as an excuse to cheaply get rid of those old houses in the way of new developments.

The value of conservation and the preservation of old buildings was finally officially recognised in the early 1970s. Demolition was slowed but by no means halted, as can be seen in this final chapter. This era saw the establishment of both Canterbury Archaeological Trust and the City Council's Conservation Department. At the same time, modern architectural styles were shunned in favour of new buildings designed in a vernacular pastiche, sometimes not very well done and, in many cases, vastly over scale. This 'change of heart' is as much to do with the pragmatic recognition of the value of tourism, as it is with the renewed appreciation for our architectural and historic past.

Canterbury has undergone many changes in the last hundred years, many not for the better. Most of these have been recorded by photographers whose work can be found within the pages of this volume. Further changes are planned, including the virtual eradication of the modern buildings of early post-war Canterbury, both good and bad. Therefore it is the responsibility of we modern historians to continue the photographic recording process for future generations.

One

Before the Blitz

Canterbury Cathedral seen from across the Waverley Football Club Grounds in 1935. In the foreground, Invicta Motors are putting new Ford saloon cars through their paces following a Concours D'Elegance along the main street. Beyond are the houses of Wincheap Green (see also page 31), the tannery (left) and gas works on the right (also pictured on page 30). Today, Telephone House can be found on the football club site and can be seen on page 119.

An East Kent Leyland TS7 coach accelerates up Summer Hill and away from Canterbury on an express service to London in the mid 1930s. No other traffic is evident and the only people visible are a couple walking their dog. Summer Hill is part of the old A2 and links Canterbury to the ancient village of Harbledown, situated behind the camera.

The city end of London Road from the junction with St Dunstan's Street and Whitstable Road in 1941 (see also page 65). The five three-storey houses in the foreground were built at various times during the late Georgian period, from the mid eighteenth-century plain facade of number 1 (nearest the camera) to the Regency stucco and bay windows of numbers 4 and 5. The jettied frontage of numbers 8 and 9 represent the old order.

The top end of St Dunstan's Street, also in 1941. To the right, numbers 39 to 44 are timber framed cottages, all but two updated with eighteenth-century front elevations. St Dunstan's House is in the centre and Swoffer & Co, fruit merchants, just visible to the left. The latter would be destroyed towards the end of the Blitz (see page 65).

St Dunstan's Street seen from the Westgate in the 1920s. Furthest right is part of the three-storey eighteenth-century furniture depository of Kennett & Sons. This would be demolished at the end of the 1940s. Beyond the North Lane junction are buildings that survive today, including the Falstaff Hotel, also pictured on page 85.

Above: Patrons of The Falstaff Tap pose for the camera across North Lane just prior to a charabanc outing in about 1929. Note the one lady present in the centre of the gathering. Also of interest is the early Georgian building to the left of the pub, the premises of coach builders Welsh Bros. It would become a Blitz victim. The timber-framed buildings on the left are also now gone, as can be seen on page 85.

Left: The Blue Anchor public house at 25 North Lane in the early 1930s (also pictured on page 102). The pub, although much altered, was part of a long range of two-storey fifteenth-century dwellings. Left is a single-storey early nineteenth-century building, occupied by Albert Sims, bootmaker, followed by a three-storey house of similar date. Both were pulled down in the early post-war years.

Old houses in North Lane and adjacent to the River Stour in the early 1930s. The jettied timber-framed pair in the centre is part of the same range as the Blue Anchor pictured opposite. These houses (numbers 31 and 32), along with the building next to the river (left), would be demolished in the late 1930s as part of an extensive slum clearance programme. The two brick houses (right) survive today and can be seen on page 102.

An aerial view of the North Lane, St Stephen's Road area, in about 1931. Centre view is the massive East Kent bus garage complex, built in two stages between 1925 and 1930 (see page 98). Bottom of the picture are the allotments and industrial buildings of St Stephen's Fields, followed by the extensive West Station coal yard sidings (see page 103).

Tower House, just off St Peter's Place in the early 1930s. The original Jacobean house had been built onto a surviving square bastion from the city wall. Two outer wings were added in the 1870s. In 1936, the house and its extensive grounds would be given to the city by the Williamson family. The grounds then became Westgate Gardens. The Victorian wings were subsequently demolished.

Houses on the west side of St Peter's Place in 1941, just prior to the removal of railings for war salvage. They were built in the 1830s as part of a large development of Regency-style artisan houses. Note that at least two of the properties are empty and boarded up. This is indicative of wartime evacuation rather than impending demolition.

Most of the east side of St Peter's Place seen in 1941. Prominent is the three-storey Oddfellows Arms Public House, run by Mr William Dunk. In 1941 the residents lost their railings. In the early 1960s, they lost their front gardens when the street was widened and linked into the new ring road (see page 128).

The bus station on the east side of St Peter's Place in about 1939. The 'Road Car Station' had been at this location since 1922. Nearest the camera is a Leyland TD4 of 1936, a type that would be rebodied in the early post-war years (see page 98). To its left is an ex-Isle Of Thanet double decker, absorbed into the company in 1937.

Above: A 1900s view of the Westgate from the St Peter's Place junction (see page 98). Note the surrounding shrubs and railings, all to be lost for salvage in 1941. To its right is the nineteenth-century Gothic police station at the top of Pound Lane. Closer observation will reveal a policeman standing outside. Part of Barrett's premises in St Peter's Street can be seen far right.

Left: An interesting group of shop buildings on the south side of St Peter's Street in the 1920s. The large eighteenth-century building houses the wool shop of Edward Lefevre. To the right is toy dealer F.C. Snell at number 46 St Peter's Street. Both shops would be demolished in 1953, following a minor fire.

Above: The Burghmote Horn is being blown following the proclamation of the accession to the throne of King George VI on 12 December 1936. The declaration was made by the Deputy Mayor, Councillor Charles Lefevre, who is standing behind the horn-blowing Town Sargent. Other dignitaries in front of the Westgate include Canon Crum (far left) and Chief Constable George Hall, second from the right.

Right: Another group of shop buildings in St Peter's Street, which, unlike those on the opposite page, survive today. On the left is a fine example of sixteenth-century vernacular architecture, the premises of antique dealer Clifford Wheeler. Right is the Oporto Tavern, an eighteenth-century timber-framed building with a mathematical tile-front elevation, similar to the Lefevre shop on the opposite page.

Left: Mrs Kemp in the doorway of her tiny cottage at 24 St Peter's Lane in the late 1920s. Her grandson Stan recalls that her prize possessions were two polished gun shells from the Great War, which she kept on the hearth in the front room. In 1933, Mrs Kemp fell ill and, after a brief spell in hospital, went to live with her son at 2 Cotton Mill Row. She died in their front room in 1934.

Below: Part of the rear elevation of the long terrace of humble cottages at 8 to 34 St Peter's Lane. This is part of an eighteenth-century development that could once be found on both sides of the lane. This, the east side of the lane, once fell within the precinct walls of Blackfriars. It then became a garden area until the houses were built.

Right: Another of Stan's relatives, his aunt, Mrs Harwood on the step of her cottage at 28 St Peter's Lane. She was next-door-but-one to Stan's grandmother. Mrs Harwood had lived here since at least the early 1920s and would remain until being forced to move out prior to demolition in 1936/1937. A third relative of Stan's also lived in the lane. She was Mrs Curd, his father's cousin.

Below: The frontages of 28 down to 12 St Peter's Lane in 1935. By this time, Mrs Kemp had died, but Mrs Harwood (whose front door is pictured far left) was still in residence. All the eighteenth-century houses on the lane's east side were designated 'Clearance Area Number 11' in a massive pre-war slum clearance programme. Demolition occurred in 1938.

Left: The former Refectory of the Dominican Blackfriars at the end of the nineteenth century. At this time, the much altered building was in use as a Unitarian Chapel. The Blackfriars Church had been demolished following the Dissolution of the Monasteries in 1538. The remaining buildings survived and were later converted into a weaving factory for Walloon refugees. Most were then demolished prior to residential redevelopment of the area (see page 67).

Below: The lofty wooden premises of fellmongers Green & Co, just off The Friars in the mid 1930s. A fellmonger was the middle stage between the abbattoir and tannery. He cleaned and prepared the animal skins: a smelly business for the centre of a Cathedral City! However, by the 1930s, the buildings were used mainly as a wool store. Note the many fleeces.

Right: A charming scene from 1932 showing a statue, thought to represent the founder of The Order of Blackfriars, St Dominic. Left is the stone steps leading up to the recently restored Refectory (see page 67). It had been saved from demolition by Mr W.H. Powell. On the opposite side of the River Stour is the only other surviving Blackfriars building, the former Guest Hall, in a near derelict state and prior to its own restoration.

Below: This picture, taken from Friars Bridge in 1941, pulls together all the elements of the three preceding views. Right, are the former fellmonger buildings, by now taken over by the British Wool Marketing Board. Far left is the Blackfriars Guest Hall with lancet windows restored. Far right can just be seen the Refectory, which is also shown on page 80. The wooden wool store burnt to the ground in the June 1942 Blitz (see page 81).

Left: The King's Head public house at 32 Northgate Street in 1941, when the publican was Mr Percival Dibbs. This is a much altered sixteenth or seventeenth-century timber-framed building that would have originally looked very much like the Christopher Marlowe house seen on page 2. It closed in the 1950s and today is the headquarters of the Canterbury Samaritans.

Below: The patchy brickwork of numbers 63 to 65 New Ruttington Lane, photographed in the mid 1930s. They were part of an early nineteenth-century development for the families of soldiers stationed at the nearby barracks (see page 62). These three houses were situated immediately behind three others (numbers 60 to 62) on the street frontage. All six were demolished as 'Slum Clearance Area No 8' at the end of the 1930s.

The butcher, Mr F.R. Beaney, poses outside his shop in his pony and trap. It is probably the 1920s, a time when such modes of transport could still be seen on the streets of Canterbury. The butcher's shop is standing on the corner of Military Road with Artillery Street. It would be pulled down in 1960.

The Royal Dragoon public house at 100 Military Road in 1941, when the publican was Mr William Ballard. It stands at the city end of the road, adjacent to the remote burial ground for St Mary Northgate. The roof would be badly damaged in the 1942 Blitz and replaced by one with a steeper pitch. When Northgate was subject to post-war demolition, several pubs were spared. Fortunately, The Royal Dragoon was one of them.

Left: Number 5 St Peter's Street on the corner with All Saints Lane in about 1920. Soon, it would be taken over by Maltby's Ltd as a car showroom: an overly optimistic ambition for such a small building. Not surprisingly, Maltby's subsequently moved to purpose built premises in New Dover Road (see page 127). Number 5 and its timber-framed neighbour were badly damaged by fire in the late 1970s. They were later rebuilt.

Below: A splendid view looking north from Kingsbridge in the early years of this century. On the left, the sixteenth-century 'Weavers House' had recently been extended back by two bays. The old weather boarded riverside warehouse housed Ellenor, the carriage builders, and above, Samuel Caldwell's glazing workshop (see page 82).

Above: The rear of the Elizabethan extension to Eastbridge Hospital from the River Stour in 1941, looking north. The river is navigable beneath the hospital and Kingsbridge, then further on to Friars Bridge and beyond. To the right is part of the recently constructed telephone exchange and, left, the rear garden of the hospital's Masters Lodge.

Right: Number 29 High Street, a Regency period building on the corner with Stour Street. Just to the right is the Main Post Office, followed by Eastbridge Hospital and Kingsbridge (see page 92). Sometime between the wars, two original round-topped ground-floor windows were knocked out in favour of this rather austere oblong one. In more recent years, two period-style windows, albeit rectangular-headed ones, have been restored by Anthony Swaine.

Left: Three delightful early post-mediaeval timber-framed houses on the east side of Stour Street. Nearest the camera is the sweet shop run by Miss Kate Fuller, in a mid seventeenth-century building. The pair of houses with the recently exposed timbers are sixteenth-century and are the homes of John Clinker (number 72) and Miss E. Westfield (number 73). The sweet shop and number 72 would be flattened in the Blitz and number 73 demolished shortly after.

Below: The Poor Priests' Hospital on the west side of Stour Street in 1941. This famous building dates from the fourteenth century, but owes much of its external appearance to post-mediaeval alterations. A flint boundary wall had recently been demolished to allow the front yard to be used as a car park. Inside could be found Canterbury Public Heath Department and the St John Ambulance Association.

Above: A splendid watercolour executed by local artist Mr E.A. Phipson in 1888, showing two ancient houses in Stour Street. However, artistic licence has been used as they were not side by side. Left is an elaborate timber-framed house that once graced the top end of Stour Street and was demolished long ago to make way for an extension to the tannery buildings. The seventeenth-century house to the right survives today opposite the junction with Hospital Lane.

Right: A cart horse pulling a load of either hay, straw or thatch, waits patiently in Church Lane St Mildred's, sometime in the 1920s. The three-storey eighteenth-century and two-storey nineteenth-century houses on the lane's west side can be seen left. All would become victims of post-war demolition. Further from the camera is part of St Mildred's Tannery at the top end of Stour Street.

The far end of Wincheap Street in the early 1930s, with only bicycles and a few parked cars in evidence. The stuccoed nineteenth-century terrace on the left survives today, but the rest of the scene has undergone dramatic changes. Beyond the cottages is the entrance to Woodville Homes (demolished in the 1950s), followed by the familiar perimeter wall and railings to Thannington Pumping Station. At the far end, the houses in Thannington would become victims of the Canterbury Bypass in the late 1970s.

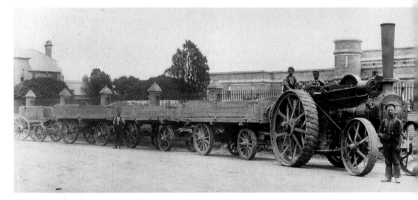

A traction-engine-hauled road train outside Thannington Pumping Station sometime at the end of the nineteenth century. The engine, wagons and water cart are owned and run by Canterbury contractors G.F. Finn. A young Robert Brett worked for Finn before setting up on his own. Behind is part of the original water works of 1869. This is the building containing the settling tanks. It was demolished together with its tower in 1994.

An aerial view of the water-pumping station and surrounding area in the mid 1920s. It is at this point that Wincheap (right) becomes Thannington (left). Before very long, council houses would be built on the hop fields and allotments to the left. Robert Brett's Wincheap depot can be seen opposite the water works. Note the pumping station's tall chimney, indicating that power was being provided by steam.

Another well-known Canterbury firm was hauliers C & G Yeoman, run by brothers Charles and George. The driver of one of their early Dennis lorries poses for the camera outside the pumping station shortly after the Great War. Yeoman's had premises in Wincheap Street, a depot just off Wincheap Grove and offices at the top of Castle Street (see page 108). They were nationalised in 1949.

A fascinating cityscape from the top of the castle ruins in the autumn of 1932. It was taken by Mr Mann of the City Council's Surveyors Department prior to the castle keep's consolidation and repair. Until recently it had been used as a coal store for the nearby gas works, seen beyond the castle's north wall (see page 122). Reparation of the keep was carried out by City Surveyor Mr H.M. Enderby.

The Norman Castle Hotel at 37 Castle Street in about 1930. This small hotel run by William Fagg is seen here from the rear, with the city wall on the right and castle keep immediately to the left. The City Surveyor's refurbishment programme also included the clearance of 'modern' buildings from the castle grounds. Consequently, the hotel was demolished in the 1930s.

Right: Another building cleared from the castle grounds was this tiny chapel in Gas Street, that stood in the shadow of the gas works. In 1875, when the Presbyterians broke away from the Congregational Church, this chapel became their place of worship. A larger and more permanent Presbyterian Church was later built in nearby Wincheap Green. Today, the only trace of the tiny chapel is some remains adhering to the rear of the adjacent oast house.

Below: A truncated stretch of the city wall bordering the castle grounds, photographed in 1941 from the site of the Norman Castle Hotel. Just beyond are the early to mid nineteenth-century houses of Wincheap Grove (see pages 9 and 109). Further along, the city wall disappears completely above ground for many hundreds of yards. This can be blamed on parliamentary troops who breached the wall in several places during the Civil War.

Numbers 1 and 2 St Margaret's Street in the early 1930s. These late sixteenth or early seventeenth-century timber-framed buildings are on the junction with Watling Street. Number 2 (left) is Fowler Brothers Dairy, whilst number 1 is empty. However, a German couple soon moved in and set up an excellent bakers shop. Sadly, with the outbreak of the Second World War, they were forced to move out.

The imposing Regency frontage of The Royal Fountain Hotel on the east side of St Margaret's Street at the turn of the twentieth century. This stuccoed brick facade hid a range of older buildings and many ancient timbers could be found inside. The large front entrance led into a passage through to extensive stables and a depot for horse-drawn buses. The hotel was utterly destroyed in the June Blitz (see page 49).

Above: The Royal Fountain Hotel from the rear courtyard in the early 1930s. By this time the stables, beneath the older wing to the left, had gone and been replaced by garage space for cars. The prefix 'Royal' was on account of Queen Victoria who stayed here 'on many occasions'. Once, whilst visiting as a child, a maid who had kissed her was scolded by Victoria's mother who did not want her child to catch a common germ!

Right: The many varied buildings on the corner of The Parade and St Margaret's Street (right). Standing right at the junction is a large scale mediaeval timber-framed building, one of a number built in the city as inns for pilgrims visiting the Becket Shrine. In 1941 it was occupied by clothiers J. Hepworth & Sons. In the early post-war years, its demolition was proposed to ease the junction. Fortunately, this never went ahead.

Left: The Corn Exchange and Longmarket on the north side of St George's Street, the city's finest Regency Period. This picture dates from around the turn of the twentieth century. The Longmarket was a long open space on the ground floor, where many individual trading stalls could be found. The Corn Exchange was situated on the floor above. Sadly, the building would fall victim to enemy bombs and an indifferent City Council (see page 50).

Below: A well-known photograph of the top end of St George's Street in Edwardian times. However, this print has been made from the original glass plate negative, recently rediscovered. St George's church is the dominant building at this end of the street. This scene would be almost completely changed by the Blitz of 1 June 1942, after which the gutted church would be one of the only structures left standing on the street's north side. The south side, on the left of the picture, would be completely wiped out, as can be seen on page 69.

Above: The inside of St George's church in the 1900s, looking along the central aisle towards the altar and chancel window. The aisle arcade arches, chancel and complete north aisle (left) date from the rebuilding work of the early 1870s (see page 71). The central aisle roof and south aisle (right) are mediaeval. Note the gas lamps and organ in the north aisle (later removed to the west gallery).

Right: Shop buildings on the north side of St George's Street in the late 1920s. At this time, individual buildings were being modernised, or, in some cases, completely replaced. Left is the newly built premises for Barclay's Bank, a copy of an older style. Centre right is Biggleston's former premises at number 22. It would shortly be pulled down to make way for a modern shop (Dolcis Shoe Co). All would be lost in the Blitz, except the lower part of Barclay's Bank (see page 94).

Canterbury South Railway Station and coal siding from the nearby footbridge in 1936. The Elham Valley Line, of which the South Station is part, opened on 1 July 1889. The railway was not successful and had been reduced to a single track in 1931. In 1940, the line would be closed to passengers and handed over to the military in response to the threat of invasion.

Another 1936 view of the South Station's coal yard, seen in the opposite direction. The iron footbridge to Nackington is at the far end beyond the coal wagons. Looming up behind the telegraph poles and loading gauges is the massive concrete frame of the new Kent and Canterbury Hospital, with construction well in progress. The new hospital would replace the old buildings in Longport (see page 40).

The new hospital complex from Ethelbert Road in the summer of 1937. The building in the current art deco or 'international moderne' style was begun in 1935 and completed at the end of the following year. Its plan consisted of an inner triangle of corridors with three projecting wings. The Z-shaped nurses home block (left) is linked to the main building by a bridge over the rear access road from Nackington Road.

On Wednesday 14 July 1937 the Duke and Duchess of Kent came to Canterbury for the official opening of the new hospital. Archbishop Cosmo Lang and Princess Marina lead a group of dignitaries along the main drive from Ethelbert Road to the hospital. Music for the ceremony was provided by the Canterbury Silver Band, which included my grandfather Harry Crampton (euphonium) and great uncle Bill Crampton (cornet).

Above: Two fine Georgian houses on the north side of St George's Place in the early to mid 1930s. Together with New Dover Road, it was created in the 1790s as a new toll road for London to Dover coaching traffic. Its new houses were considered very prestigious at the time. However, by the 1930s, most of them were being converted into offices. Number 4 (left) was about to be taken over by the Isle of Thanet Building Society and number 5 was about to become a doctor's surgery (see page 114).

Left: The office premises of Robert Brett & Sons Ltd. at 16 St George's Place, decorated to celebrate the accession to the throne of George VI in early 1937. Brett's depot was at the top end of Wincheap, opposite the pumping station (see page 29). Their office premises would be destroyed by fire, along with most of St George's Place on 1 June 1942 (see page 59).

Right: Members of staff at Robert Brett's St George's Place offices pose for the camera on the first floor balcony in 1937. They are (back row, left to right): Tony Taylor, Ted Tritton and Jackie Burt; (front row, left to right) Mollie Peters, Aubry Wilky and Irene Willett. At the far end of St George's Place can be seen the recently constructed Regal Cinema, also evident on page 114.

Below: The Baptist Church in the early 1900s, peeping out from behind the late Georgian houses on the south side of St George's Place. It had been built in 1863 on a vacant, if somewhat cramped, plot. However, just prior to the Great War, the church authority purchased and demolished the houses on either side. To the left, a new Church Hall (opened in 1914) was built. On the right, the forecourt was extended and a matching turret added to the church.

Above: An aerial view of the St Augustine's Abbey and Longport area in about 1930. Just right of centre and surrounded by the abbey ruins is the old Kent and Canterbury Hospital (see page 75). Along the bottom is Longport Street, much of which would be lost in the Blitz (see page 99). Top left is the abbey's fourteenth-century Findon Gate, adjacent to the junction for Monastery Street and Lady Wootton's Green (see opposite).

Left: Large amounts of re-used Caen stone make up the side wall of the back garden to 30 Longport Street. This picture from August 1939 was taken from Lower Chantry Lane near its junction with Longport Street. The stone would have come from the ruins of the church building to St Augustine's Abbey which became a quarry for building materials in the years following the Dissolution of the Monasteries (see page 126).

The lower part of Findon Gate, the main entrance to St Augustine's Abbey, from Lady Wootton's Green in about 1900. Built in 1309, the gate survived the Dissolution as it was part of the abbey complex converted into a Royal Palace for Henry VIII. When the palace fell into ruin in the eighteenth century, the Findon Gate became part of a public house! It was to be badly blast damaged in the Blitz (see page 57).

The south side of Lady Wootton's Green in the mid 1930s. Nearest the camera is a much altered late mediaeval timber-framed house, by now the premises of A. Rose, furniture remover. Next is a delightful pair of mid seventeenth-century houses displaying the typical Canterbury jettied gables. The city wall beyond had recently been exposed by the demolition of Star Brewery. Both timbered houses would be devastated in the Blitz (see page 56).

Above: A large section of the south side of Burgate Street in the mid 1930s, showing some of its fine early post-mediaeval timber-framed buildings. Nearest the camera is the rear gateway to the Corn Exchange and Longmarket (see page 34). Adjacent is one of the shops run by Court Bros Ltd, house furnishers. This particular one (50 Burgate Street) is the Ideal Homes and Gardens Shop (see page 51).

Left: A naked nymph, sporting a 1920s bob, converses with a frog at the edge of a small ornamental pond in Canterbury's lost garden. This charming oasis could be found behind numbers 50 to 52 Burgate street. The garden and its structures are thought to have been the responsibility of Percy Court himself. It stretched back from Burgate Street and ran parallel to the single-storey rear section of the Longmarket complex (right).

Right: Another captivating picture of the lost garden. This view was taken at the far end, and adjacent to a small detached building where various crafts could be purchased. The polished globe reflects a distorted image of the backs of the properties along Burgate street. Note the china cat on the wishing well, stalking the tiny china bird above. The Blitz obliterated this garden completely. Today, the site is part of a lorry unloading area off Iron Bar Lane (see page 107).

Below: The blast-damaged south side of Burgate Street following the lunchtime hit-and-run raid of Thursday 11 October 1940. A direct hit destroyed a number of shops opposite and killed nine people. War damage assessor Anthony Swaine can be seen up the ladder against the Burgate Farm House Tearooms. All the buildings featured here were repaired, only to be completely destroyed in the main Blitz of 1 June 1942.

Above: The Buttermarket and Christ Church Gate seen from Mercery Lane at the end of the last century. The gate was built in the early sixteenth century and was the Cathedral's last major building project prior to the Reformation. Today, the Buttermarket would be teaming with foreign tourists. One hundred years ago, there were just a few local people going about their business. The woman on the left is pushing a small milk cart.

Left: A close up study of Christ Church Gate in 1904, showing the external stonework in a very poor condition. The gate has suffered over the years. It was vandalised by parliamentary troops in 1643, who tore down the statue of Christ from the niche above the entrance arch and burned its large wooden doors. In 1803, its twin turrets were dismantled to enable Alderman James Simmons to see the Cathedral clock from his High Street bank premises!

Right: The newly restored gate at its unveiling ceremony on 19 June 1937. By 1931, the gate's disintegration had become so advanced that the Friends of Canterbury Cathedral undertook to finance its complete restoration (see page 83). The gate, less the turrets, had been finished by 1935 and unveiled by Archbishop Cosmo Lang on 22 June of that year. The rebuilding of the turrets took two more years.

Below: Numerous awe-struck clergymen and freemasons in the Buttermarket, their heads turned upwards, for the moment when the newly rebuilt turrets for Christ Church Gate are unveiled. The ceremony is being conducted by Dr George Bell, one time Dean of Canterbury, and, by then, Bishop of Chichester. The current Dean, Hewlett Johnson, is just below centre, flanked by two small choir boys.

Left: The Cathedral's magnificent Bell Harry Tower, under restoration in the early 1900s. Many hundreds of lengths of wooden scaffolding have been lashed together for this purpose. As with Christ Church Gate, the reason for restoration was its crumbling external stonework. Tons of Doulting stone were brought down from Northampton to be used on the tower. To this day, the 'new' material has still not blended in with the original Caen stone.

Below: The ivy-clad remains of the Cathedral's Infirmary Chapel and Chancel (far end) in the 1880s. After the Dissolution, many of the surviving Christ Church Priory buildings were divided up amongst the various stalls of the new Dean and Chapter. The Infirmary Hall and Chancel were allotted to Stall One, with the exception of the central aisle, which was de-roofed to become the Brick Walk.

The west wall of the Cathedral Library and mediaeval Chapter House (right) above the eastern cloister walk in the late nineteenth century. The Victorian rose window and gable of the library building is sitting upon an arcade of eleventh-century Romanesque arches that once formed part of the priory's Great Dorter or Dormitory. Most of the library building would be destroyed in the June 1942 Blitz (see page 53).

The Deanery with part of its front wall blasted away following the lunchtime hit-and-run raid on Wednesday 17 October 1940. A formation of Messerschmitts had made a deliberate attack on the Cathedral. Canon Banks' house in the South Precincts was destroyed and another bomb left this crater right in front of the Deanery. Fortunately, no lives were lost on that day.

Left: A fine photographic study of the Cathedral taken from the roof of Lefevre's new premises on the east side of Guildhall Street in 1932. The roofs and chimneys of properties in Sun Street crowd together in the foreground. The twin western towers were, in fact, built 400 years apart. The South West Tower (right) superseded its Norman predecessor in the 1430s, but the eleventh-century North West Tower was not replaced until 1832.

Below: The Cathedral taken at 800 feet from an RAF bomber in the late 1930s. The Cathedral's glass is still in-situ, which dates it to before 1938 and the Munich Crisis. In the foreground are the houses in the South Precincts and shop buildings on both sides of Burgate Street. Everything in the bottom right hand corner would be wiped out by a four ton bomb in June 1942 (see page 55).

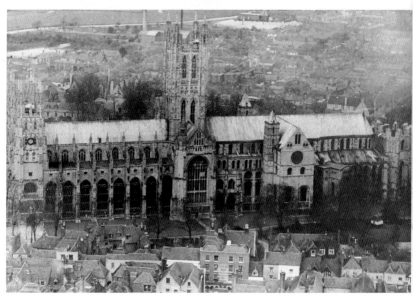

Two

The Blitz of 1942
and its Aftermath

Members of the National Fire Service damp down the smouldering remains of the Royal Fountain Hotel in St Margaret's Street (see page 32). It is the morning of 1 June 1942, only hours after the infamous Baedeker Raid that devastated much of the south east quadrant of the city. Beyond is the Freemason's Tavern, which, although damaged and later half demolished, would continue to trade (see page 96).

The Rose Club, formerly The Rose Hotel, the only building in The Parade to be affected by the raid of 1 June. Although the brick-built Regency facade survives, much of the earlier timber-framed interior has been lost. As a consequence, the entire structure would soon be demolished. Beyond are the other buildings on the south side of The Parade, familiar to most people today.

The north side of St George's Street, with firemen bringing the many incendiary fires under control. Dominating the scene is the attractive Regency facade of the Corn Exchange and Longmarket building (see page 34). Despite the devastation on either side, it stands remarkably intact, with only its roof and part of the interior lost. Nevertheless, the demolition gangs would soon move in (see page 52).

Bewildered shop and office workers survey the changed scene in Burgate Street. 1 June 1942 was a Monday morning and many people who came to work in the city were genuinely unaware of the extent of the devastation they were to find. Right is the intact rear entrance gate to the Corn Exchange and Longmarket complex. To its left, an iron joist is all that is left of Courts Homes and Gardens shop (see page 42).

A helmeted policeman prevents people from entering St George's Place, because of an unexploded bomb in the carriageway. The tottering walls of its once impressive late Georgian buildings, including Robert Brett's Office (far left), provide a dramatic backdrop (see page 38). Far right, a woman with a dog and pram picks her way through the rubble at the junction with Lower Chantry Lane (see page 115).

A fine profile of Prince George, Duke of Kent, taken during his visit to the Blitz-torn city on 4 June 1942. The Duke and his entourage were accompanied by Canterbury dignitaries, including the Mayor Charles Lefevre. Behind the Duke are some ancient cottages in Northgate Street showing signs of blast damage.

Right: The Duke chats to demolition workers grouped ominously in front of the gutted shell of the Corn Exchange and Longmarket building (see page 50). To his left, Alderman Lefevre glances over at members of the Duke's entourage. Within days of the royal visit, the impressive neo-classical frontage of this building would be no more (see page 106).

Right: The Cathedral, undoubtedly the Luftwaffe's principal target, had a remarkable escape from any serious damage. The Victorian Library, the Cathedral's only casualty, is pictured here shortly after its destruction. Other former monastic buildings badly damaged included the Larder Gate, Forrens Gate and the Deanery (see page 47).

Below: Members of the armed forces pick their way through the remains of the Cathedral's nineteenth-century library building shortly after its direct hit. The Victorian work seen here and in the picture above, cleverly imitates the Romanesque style of the monastic Dorter, whose ruins the library encompassed. Fortunately, none of the original eleventh-century remains were destroyed (see page 82).

Left: A barrage balloon hovering high above the city, captured through one of the Cathedral's shattered stained-glass windows. It had long been realised that Canterbury was a target in the so-called Baedeker series of raids (named after the German guidebooks), although it was not until the day after the main raid of 1 June 1942 that the balloons were rushed to the city.

Below: The blast damaged stone altar of St Anselm's Chapel on the south side of the Cathedral. Only yards away, a four ton bomb that just missed the Cathedral had caused a huge crater in the South Precincts. Had most of the Cathedral's precious stained-glass not been removed and stored prior to hostilities, then the blast damage would have been far worse.

Right: A scene of devastation surrounds the 20ft deep crater in the Cathedral's South Precincts and Burgate Street. By this time, camouflage netting had been stretched across the void. In the foreground are the remains of a seventeenth-century building on the north side of Burgate Street (see page 48). Beyond the crater is the remaining half of Canon Crum's house (see pages 78 and 79).

Below: Another part of the devastated South Precincts, as seen from the Cathedral. Beyond the nineteenth-century wall, badly blast-damaged trees hang on to their few remaining leaves. Below the shattered limbs are the Blitzed ruins of a mediaeval building known as The Plumbary. The massive bomb crater is just off picture to the right.

A twisted jumble of timbers is all that remains of one fifteenth and two seventeenth-century houses on the south side of Lady Wootton's Green (see page 41). However, what we see here is not only the work of the Luftwaffe, but also that of the demolition gangs. The sturdy oak frames of two of the houses still stood upright following the Baedeker Raid, but fell victim to the thorough post-Blitz clearance operations.

A close up study of part of the timber frame to the fifteenth-century house at number 4 Lady Wootton's Green. This picture was taken after demolition workers had collapsed the upstanding upper storey and roof timbers, but such was this building's strength that the lower storey survived even this process. Note the mediaeval dragon beam and curved corner bracket nearest the camera.

The blast-damaged Findon Gate from Lady Wootton's Green in mid June 1942. The gateway survived the dissolution of St Augustine's Abbey and served various functions until eventually becoming part of St Augustine's College (see page 41). The damage would be repaired in the late 1940s. Not so lucky are the devastated cottages at numbers 2 to 4 Lady Wootton's Green, far left. Complete demolition swiftly followed.

This fine eighteenth-century house on the north side was the only dwelling in Lady Wootton's Green to be retained and repaired after the Blitz. The house had been built onto the remains of the Abbey's Almonry Chapel. A recent architectural survey of the building revealed that much mediaeval fabric exists buried beneath the Georgian brick and plaster work (see page 87).

Left: A young lad surveys the pile of rubble and timbers that was once a row of early nineteenth-century shops in Lower Bridge Street. This damage was caused by high explosive bombs and resulted in loss of life. The half surviving building to the right is the premises of J. Hoare, greengrocer. Beyond and to the left, Zoar Chapel, set in the city wall, is just visible.

Below: Mr W. Fisk-Moore's photograph of the rear of his own smouldering premises, taken at dawn on 1 June 1942. This is, or was, his studio at 7 St George's Place. He lost all his photographic equipment and an irreplaceable archive of negatives. His famous Blitz pictures were taken using the mug-shot camera borrowed from the police station.

The ruinous office premises of Robert Brett & Sons Ltd at number 16 St George's Place in mid June 1942 (see page 51). The demolition crane has already attacked the building, the first priority being to remove any walls thought to be dangerous and thus allow the main thoroughfares to be re-opened.

The remains of numbers 12 to 15 St George's Place, seen from the intact buildings opposite. Workmen tidy up the rubble created by the recent actions of the demolition crane. Later, it would return to level the site completely. The surviving ground floor stone facade once belonged to the Pearl Assurance Company.

Above: The gutted, yet reasonably intact, interior of St Mary Bredin church in Rose Lane during July 1942. The photographer is standing in the central aisle and looking through the north aisle arcade towards the west wall (see page 125). Through the window can be seen the completely intact St Margaret's church in nearby St Margaret's Street.

Left: A badly damaged wall monument in the north aisle of St Mary Bredin church, also pictured in July 1942. This mural tablet was dedicated to Sir Christopher Mann who died in 1638. The Mann family coat of arms are displayed at the top. The gutted shell of St Mary Bredin's was demolished in the autumn of 1942.

Right: Numbers 18 and 19 Watling Street, an impressive pair of Jacobean houses gutted in the June Blitz. Quite exceptionally, they escaped the attention of the demolition gangs and continued in use as an analytical chemist's premises, beneath a temporary ground floor roof constructed within the shell. Sadly, their luck would run out in 1953 when they were pulled down to create an open car parking space.

Below: The top end of Watling Street following the daylight raid of 31 October 1942. Centre view, workmen demolish the last standing remains of the Congregational Church. It had been gutted by incendiary bombs earlier in June, then, unluckily, fell victim to the October raiders (see page 73). Just visible right is the Dane John Tavern, to be pulled down in the late 1940s.

The area around the four-ton bomb crater from the Cathedral in July 1942, also pictured on page 55. In the foreground, the remains of Canon Crum's house awaits demolition. Just beyond, the crater itself is being filled with demolition rubble brought in from clearance operations across the city. A large roofless depository in Iron Bar Lane awaits its fate (see page 79).

A cityscape showing Northgate, a part of Canterbury largely untouched by the June Blitz. Military Road in the centre, runs straight to the army barracks at the top of the picture. This area is covered by streets crowded with terraced houses built in the early nineteenth century to serve the barracks (see page 22). Northgate would be subject to extensive slum clearance from the late 1950s onwards.

Three

The Late 1940s –
The Buddleia Years

Above: Canterbury and its Cathedral, taken in 1946 from the fields to the north of the city, where the university now stands. The start of the post-war rebuilding was still five years away. In the meantime, down in the Blitzed areas, wild flowers, tree saplings and Buddleia consolidated their hold, checked only by the occasional activities of the amateur archaeologists.

Above: St Thomas' Hill in 1948, to the north of the city and on the main route to Whitstable and the coast. The road is deserted save for an East Kent bus on a city service to either Blean or Rough Common. The Cathedral can just be seen behind the row of Scots Pines. At the bottom of the hill is the St Dunstan's suburb.

Left: Derelict early nineteenth-century cottages in New Street in the late 1940s. This appears to be bomb damage, which could be found sporadically across the St Dunstan's suburb. The exception was the Station Road West junction area, where destruction was total. These cottages were never destined to be repaired and demolition occurred shortly after this picture was taken.

Above: Two gentlemen watch an approaching bus near the junction of Whitstable Road, St Dunstan's Street and London Road (see page 10). On the left are the eighteenth-century cottages at numbers 2 to 8 Whitstable Road, before the shop fronts intruded. Just beyond the lamp-post is the Monument public house at 37 St Dunstan's Street, the publican being George Wenham.

Right: The top end of St Dunstan's Street in 1949. Prominent is St Dunstan's House, a building with an interesting architectural history. Hidden behind the mid-eighteenth-century frontage are the substantial remains of a mediaeval structure. To its left is the newly built warehouse for fruit merchants Swoffer & Co. Their previous premises were destroyed on 22 January 1944, during one of the last raids on Canterbury (see page 11).

Left: Canterbury's famous leaning building, the Kings School Shop in 1949. It dates from 1647, but it was not until the nineteenth century that the structure acquired its famous lean. This is thought to have been caused by overly ambitious alterations to the chimney stack, which resulted in it settling in a northerly slant and pulling the timber frame out of true.

Below: Another view of the Kings School Shop building, this time taken from Knotts Lane and looking across the top end of Kings Street. Note the extremely plain un-jettied rear elevation, compared to those facades facing onto the street. Until recently, the empty fenced off site in the foreground was occupied by a group of empty seventeenth and eighteenth-century buildings fronting King Street. They had been pulled down in 1946.

Right: Number 20 King Street, a late seventeenth-century house and formerly a pub called The Farriers Arms. The four large Regency windows in the front elevation had replaced eight original Georgian ones. These would be restored in the mid 1960s by Anthony Swaine. Right are the twin obelisks that flank the entrance to the synagogue. Furthest right is a stuccoed late Georgian house (number 21), followed by Jackson's scrap-yard.

Below: The north end of the former Blackfriars Refectory, just prior to the complete rebuilding of the gable end wall. At this time, the building was used as the Christian Scientist Church. Prior to the 1920s, it was covered in eighteenth-century stucco, had many inserted Georgian windows and was the Unitarian Chapel (see page 20). Restoration work had been supervised by Charles Moore.

The north side of St George's Street in the late 1940s, a wasteland of Buddleia-filled cellars and wall fragments. During the brief period between the Blitz and reconstruction, uninterrupted views of the Cathedral could be enjoyed from St George's Street. It was also the time when Council members and officials struggled to put together the rebuilding plans.

A study of Councillor J.G.B. Stone on a bomb site adjacent to the old Kentish Gazette print works (left). Then well into his eighties, 'Stonie' had been a council member continuously since 1899. Still active in the late 1940s, he was one of the few elected members to oppose the implementation of the original redevelopment scheme, the Holden Plan of 1945. He died in 1957, aged 94.

Elected members and officials gathered at the site of Whitefriars Gate on the south side of St George's Street (see page 34). They are looking over at St George's Church (see below). The gentleman with the glasses and umbrella is Alderman Barrett, Chairman of the City Council Town Planning Committee. To his right is Councillor Jennings, a future Mayor of Canterbury.

The gutted shell of St George's church on the street's north side, a victim of incendiary bombs. It was one of the few buildings still standing in St George's Street in the late 1940s. An attempt to demolish it two weeks after the main June 1942 raid had been halted by Canon Crum, but not before the top of the tower and part of the south wall had already been pulled down.

Above: Alderman Barrett gestures towards the mutilated remains of the south wall of St George's church. He is probably saying something like, 'the whole lot will have to come down'. The lean figure to his right is City Architect Hugh Wilson, author of the 1947 Development Plan. This was a scaled-down version of the rejected Holden Plan, which proposed far less compulsory purchase.

Left: Hugh Wilson and his colleagues turn their backs on St George's Church, both literally and metaphorically. The consensus of opinion in the City Council of the late 1940s, was that the ruins be completely demolished. Here we see the west side of the bell tower with its twelfth-century Romanesque doorway. To the left is the mediaeval west wall of the central aisle, followed by the Victorian west wall of the north aisle.

Above: The ruins of the church from the north east. Apart from the tower, much of the fabric here dates from the Victorian expansion of 1872. Nearest the camera is the east end gabled wall of the chancel. The proposed demolition of the church would have not only allowed St George's Street to be straightened out, but also provide for more space for new shops.

Right: The Victorian north wall of St George's church, containing much re-used mediaeval fabric recovered from St Mary Magdalene church. Through the window are the ruinous aisle arcades (also re-cycled fabric) followed by the surviving part of the church's mediaeval south wall (see page 35). Nothing of what we see here was destined to survive. In the end, the council compromised with the conservationists and retained just the tower.

A Catholic pilgrimage from Jerusalem comes to rest on St George's Terrace. A priest traces their journey on a giant globe, whilst other pilgrims carrying a huge wooden cross look on. St George's Terrace runs along the City Wall rampart with the cattle market and Upper Bridge Street below to the right. Before the Blitz, a row of late Georgian houses ran along the terrace to the left.

The single storey Harris' Alms Houses at numbers 12 to 17 Upper Bridge Street in the late 1940s. This delightful row was built in the late eighteenth or early nineteenth century. Note that some of the original windows have been replaced. They would be demolished in 1964 to make way for the Lombard House office development. The three-storey house on the far left survives today.

Right: An interesting study of the famous Invicta locomotive from 1946. At the time, it was in very poor condition, so much so that the city council seriously considered selling it for scrap! Local conservationists raised the alarm and after an embarrassing feature on the radio, there was a sudden official change of mind. Behind, the city wall clearly shows the affects of the Blitz. It would be repaired, only to collapse again in the early 1960s.

Below: The prefabricated Congregational Church in Watling Street, newly erected on the site of its Blitzed predecessor, in 1949 (see page 61). A permanent brick built church would be built here in the mid 1950s (see page 111). Sadly, this impressive modern structure is due to be demolished as part of the Whitefriars Development Scheme.

Above: Number 1 St Martin's Hill, a fine Georgian House, owned in 1949 by Mr Jasper Mounsey. As with 20 King Street (page 67), its original windows had been replaced by larger ones in the Regency period. Recently, the early Georgian pattern has been restored. At the end of the lane, left, is the lych gate and graveyard for St Martin's, the oldest parish church in England.

Left: The Anne and John Smith Alms Houses in Longport Street. These eight tiny dwellings, built in 1657 and in the late 1940s, still retained their original appearance. Note the tall chimneys and Dutch-style gable ends. The Princess Charlotte public house, seen on the far left, would be demolished in the 1960s for road widening, as would the alms houses' front boundary wall.

Right: The central part of the imposing Canterbury Technical College, the school my father attended, on the north side of Longport Street (see page 99). Built from 1793 onwards, the building spent nearly the first 150 years of its life as the original Kent and Canterbury Hospital (see page 40). In the 1960s, new technical schools rendered the old building obsolete once more. The whole complex was demolished in 1972.

Below: Canterbury College buildings, this time taken from the rear and looking across the ruins of St Augustine's Abbey (see page 40). This is the huge crypt of Abbot Scotland's church, which was begun in 1073. The vast majority of the church was pulled down for building materials after the abbey's dissolution.

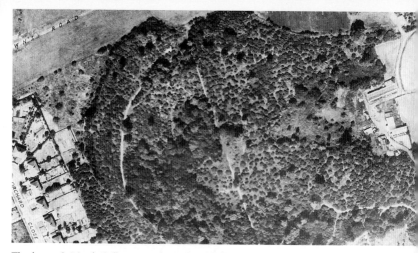

The former St Mary's College grounds on the Hales Place Estate, seen from the air in 1946. All the main buildings had been pulled down in 1928. The woodland, with its geometric walls and paths, was laid out in the mid-eighteenth century, when the Hales family built their mansion here. Later, this shape would influence the road pattern of the 1950s housing estate.

St Stephen's church in the late 1940s. It is the church of the ancient village of Hackington, an area that includes the Hales Place Estate. Much of it, including the stout Norman tower, dates from around 1100 and is a rebuilding of an earlier Saxon structure. Other portions are early English and Perpendicular Gothic, including the porch, belfry and tower buttresses.

Four

The 1950s –
The Reconstruction

November 1951 and the walls of the new Woolworth Store begin to rise on the north side of St George's Street (see page 68). This was the first new shop to appear following the implementation of the Wilson Development Plan, although other buildings had recently emerged outside of the plan's control. Woolworth's opened amidst much clamour in July 1952 (see pages 94 and 95).

Left: August 1950 and the Cathedral Dean and Chapter are about to develop the site of the filled in bomb crater on the north side of Burgate Street (see page 55). Being privately owned by the Dean and Chapter, the street's north side fell outside of the area covered by the Wilson Plan. The south side in the foreground was the city's responsibility and would be developed in the late 1950s.

Below: The new development, to be named Burgate House, nearing completion in September 1951. The whole project was funded in the greater part by the Canadian Government. The Dean and Chapter chose a rather conservative and traditional style of architecture in striking contrast to the City Council, who would bravely use modern styles for their buildings in St George's Street.

Right: The steel framework for the Dean and Chapter's new shopping development, as seen opposite, begins to take shape in the spring of 1951. This is six or more months before the City Council began to implement their official development plan. Behind, the Cathedral still waits for its ancient stained glass to be restored.

Below: Burgate House shortly after completion and uninterrupted views of the Cathedral are no more. In the foreground, tree saplings and wild flowers grow unopposed along the south side of Burgate Street. On the left, Iron Bar Lane is being used as a car park. The gentleman on the far left stands on a concreted area where once stood a huge depository building (see page 62).

Left: The fine art deco influenced frontage of The Friars Cinema in May 1951. The film on show is *The Browning Version*, starring Michael Redgrave and Jean Kent. The cinema had been built by the Odeon Company in September 1933. The name 'Friars' was used to avoid confusion with the existing Odeon Hall in St Peter's Street. Today, the frontage survives as part of the new Marlowe Theatre.

Below: A charming picture of the River Stour and The Christian Scientist church, as seen from The Friars Bridge in the early 1950s (see page 21). The three small boys are probably posing for the camera rather than intending to go sailing. The Christian Scientist church, once part of Blackfriars Friary, is featured several times in this volume (see page 67).

Right: A classic study of Canterbury Cathedral seen from the Friars Cinema. In the early post-war years, many city bomb sites were pressed into service as temporary car parks. Those in The Friars were no exception. The site in the foreground was once occupied by fellmongers Green & Co (see pages 20 and 21). Today the Friends Meeting House can be found here.

Below: The Cathedral, this time at ground level and taken from Friars Bridge. The photographer is looking down The Friars to where it meets the junctions for Best Lane (right), King Street (left) and Orange Street (straight ahead). A second Friars bomb site is being used as a car park, a situation that continued until as recently as 1996.

Above: One hundred year old Samuel Caldwell (left) holds up the last piece of stained-glass to be restored in the south west transept's main window. As the Cathedral Master Glazier, he supervised this major job throughout the early 1950s. Sam, who was the brother of Rupert Bear creator Mary Tourtel, lived to a ripe old age, dying in 1953 at the age of 102!

Left: The site of the Cathedral's Victorian Library, photographed on 8 October 1951 (see page 53). Whilst the last remains of the Blitzed building were being removed, some eleventh-century columns were discovered encased within the nineteenth-century fabric. The four columns seen here in-situ, were once at the south end of the Great Dorter, in its undercroft. Beyond is Wibert's mid twelfth-century water tower.

Above: Many beautifully hatted ladies grace the Cathedral Chapter House in June 1957. They, together with the few gentlemen amongst them, are members of The Friends Of Canterbury Cathedral, an association formed shortly after the Great War. One of their earliest and most noteworthy achievements was the complete restoration of Christ Church Gate (see pages 44 and 45).

Right: The new Cathedral Library nearing completion on 20 May 1953. Like its Victorian predecessor, the new building carefully encompassed remains of the Great Dorter, particularly its west wall. The new library was designed by John Denman in a pastiche of old architectural styles and constructed by Canterbury builders Denne & Co Ltd. It officially opened in July 1954.

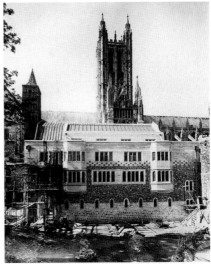

Above: Canterbury's only surviving city gate, the Westgate, causing difficulties to a large crane on a low loader in 1952. Time and time again throughout the last fifty years, this fourteenth-century gateway has frustrated the drivers of large vehicles, who try to squeeze through its narrow passageway. The crane is probably on its way to St George's Street to assist in the reconstruction.

Left: The narrowness of the gateway's ancient through passage is clearly illustrated in this wintry scene from early 1956. Beyond are buildings on either side of St Peter's Street. The ones in the foreground are soon to be demolished for the ring road proposed by the Wilson Plan. A snow covered East Kent Guy Arab double-decker from 1950 is about to pass alongside the Westgate.

Above: North Lane Car Park from the northern drum tower of the Westgate in 1956 (see page 11). Note the fine range of timber-framed buildings on the lanes west side. A similar range once existed on the car park side (see page 12), but were lost to a combination of Blitz action and early post-war demolition. North Lane was soon to be widened, reducing the car park's size.

Right: An unusual study of the Falstaff Hotel and adjacent buildings in St Dunstan's Street. The photographer is standing with his back to the Westgate. The Falstaff Inn is an interesting fifteenth-century building with seventeenth-century alterations, including the facade. Many of the adjacent properties also originate from the late mediaeval period and hide behind later frontages.

The Lower Bridge Street premises of The Invicta Motor Engineering Works Ltd in 1950. It consisted of purpose-built garages and showrooms, as well as some adapted elderly timber-framed houses. Between 1961 and 1963, the entire premises would be completely rebuilt and all the old buildings swept away. Furthest from the camera is Brickies butcher's shop (see page 126).

Two senior Invicta directors pose for the camera with their resident veteran car 'The Old Crock', in May 1950 during Canterbury Service Week. Standing alongside is the Mayor Councillor Jennings, who is shaking hands with Mr Raymond Mayes. Owner and Managing Director Major J.B. Thompson is at the wheel.

The 'Invicta Girls' in front of their float in July 1953, prior to taking part in Whitstable Carnival. The picture taken in Lady Wootton's Green, includes the surviving Georgian house also pictured on page 57. Note that the 'girl' representing Great Britain is the only one in shorts. The float won second prize at Whitstable and, later, third prize at Canterbury Carnival.

Actress and singer Miss Jessie Matthews, guest of honour at Invicta Motor's Service Week, throws a coin into an ornamental fountain. On top is the gear box from a Zephyr Six. The picture from April 1955, was taken in the showroom of the Lower Bridge Street complex. To the right of Miss Matthews is Mr A. Hall, Sales Manager of the Ford Motor Company and Invicta's Mr D.H.G. Thrush.

Left: Number 26 Castle Street, a white stuccoed early nineteenth-century house, with two-storey bow-fronted windows, so typical of the Regency period. In the early 1950s, this was the home of Mrs Cozens, with the workshops for hotel furnishers Nason's Ltd, situated behind. Just beyond is a group of more humble eighteenth-century dwellings occupying the corner into Castle Row.

Below: St Mary De Castro Gardens on a fine spring day in 1955. This charming area is so named, as it was once a graveyard for St Mary De Castro church. The photographer is standing on the actual site of this long lost building. The cottages (left) are on the west side of Castle Street and the large shop premises (right) stands on the corner with St Mary's Street.

Right: Number 68 Castle Street, one of the best houses in the street, but certainly not the oldest. The brick facades of 1847 display a transitional Georgian/Victorian style. It is thought that elements of an earlier structure can be found within. In 1952, the occupants were the same as they are today, namely the solicitors Mowll and Mowll. In the foreground is Castle Street's only bomb site, walled off for safety because of the exposed cellar.

Below: Part of the premises for Cakebread, Robey & Co Ltd at 77 and 78 Castle Street, near the bottom end. These builder's merchants also sold Calor Gas appliances and many of the cookers and fires available are displayed in this single storey showroom building. The firm would move to Wincheap Industrial Estate in 1973 and their old premises were demolished shortly afterwards.

Mr William Deedes, M.P. and Parliamentary Secretary to the Ministry of Housing (third from right), inspects a new type of council house on the London Road Estate in November 1954. Also surveying the scene is Alderman H.P. Dawton, resplendent in his mayoral chains. Standing between them and looking rather disdainful is the Town Clerk, Mr John Boyle.

The Right Hon D. Heathcoat Amory, M.P., the Minister of Agriculture and Fisheries, acts as a temporary auctioneer at the opening of the new cattle market on 12 March 1955. The Mayor Alderman Dawton (to his right) is once more in attendance. Note that at this time, the style of hat you wore very much denoted your status!

The opening of the new Red Cross Centre in Lower Chantry Lane, during March 1955. The ceremony was conducted by Archbishop Geoffrey Fisher, who can be seen centre view with his wife. Lower Chantry Lane itself saw many changes in the mid 1950s, including extensive road widening.

A champagne toast marks the opening of Southern Autos' new garage in Rose Lane during May 1959 (see page 110). The personality invited to attend the celebration is television's 'Dixon of Dock Green', Jack Warner. To his left is the firm's Managing Director, Mr J.A. Dodd. Also in attendance is the current mayor, Alderman W.S. Bean and his wife.

The west end of High Street in November 1954, with much traffic in evidence (see page 25). To describe all of Canterbury's main street as the High Street is confusing, as only this short middle stretch is actually named 'High Street'. Beyond the Kingsbridge bottleneck are the shops and buildings of St Peter's Street, another part of the continuous main street.

Eager shoppers queue outside Baldwin & Son department stores, for the annual winter sale. Baldwin's, at 32 and 33 High Street, was one of the most popular ladies outfitters in the 1950s. Their premises consisted of two late mediaeval timber-framed buildings, hidden behind a later facade and modern shop front. Baldwin's would close in the late 1960s and their buildings would be demolished.

A Salvation Army Youth parade march past senior members of their organisation in Whitehorse Lane during October 1955. The large brick built Salvation Army 'temple' is located behind the cameraman. The white-painted building on the left is the Cherry Tree public house. Far right is an old house which would disappear in the 1960s. At the far end is the junction with the High Street.

A fascinating study of a busy High Street, also to be seen on the front cover. A policeman is on point duty at the junction with Guildhall Street. At busy times, the traffic lights would be turned off and police controlled the flow. Note the remains of the old Guildhall, mostly demolished with much controversy in 1950. Buses and bicycles far outnumbered private cars in this era.

Above: A Roman Catholic procession in St George's Street, the best known part of Canterbury's main street, in the summer of 1951. The much vandalised ruins of St George's church can clearly be seen (see pages 69 to 71). The remains of the south wall had been demolished in 1951. Beyond it, the overgrown wasteland that is the north side of St George's Street, awaits imminent redevelopment.

Left: The side walls of the new Woolworth store rise above the Buddleia-filled cellars on the north side of St George's Street in November 1951 (see page 77). Far right is the tower of St George's church. Note the shattered clock face, a target for many stone-throwing small boys. In the middle distance, the truncated Barclay's Bank Hall is still trading (see page 35).

Spring 1954 and the reconstruction of St George's Street is well underway. Restoration of the church tower has begun and the first part of the colonnaded terrace of shops on the south side is complete (see page 69). Woolworth's has new neighbours, including the striking and award winning David Greig shop. Also by now, the street had been widened considerably to forty feet.

The rebuilding nearing completion in late 1955 (see page 34). The restored St George's Tower now stands free of scaffolding, although it still awaits the replacement of its repaired Victorian clock. At the far end on the north side, the new Barclay's Bank has emerged on the site of its predecessor.

Cheerful cleaning ladies help to make ready The Marlowe Theatre in St Margaret's Street for its grand opening in 1951. The theatre was converted from a former cinema, the Central Picture Theatre, which had been built from new in 1927. The conversion took seven months to complete and cost £38,000.

An external view of The Marlowe Theatre taken from St Margaret's Street and adjacent to the Marlowe car park, where once stood the Royal Fountain Hotel (see page 49). The major part of the cost of conversion was taken up by the construction of a large extension building (far left) at the stage end. Nearer the camera is the Blitz-damaged Freemason's Tavern (see page 118).

Right: A detailed study of the polygonal apsed chancel of St Margaret's church from the early 1950s. Although much of the church is fourteenth-century, what we see here is Victorian work. The original chancel projected out much further into St Margaret's Street and had to be demolished in about 1850 to effect road widening. Sir Gilbert Scott oversaw the restoration and designed this new truncated chancel end.

Below: The tiny early nineteenth-century neo-classical fish market building, hidden amongst its plainer neighbours in St Margaret's Street. By the mid 1950s, when this view was taken, it had been divided into two small shops and its classical columns concealed behind the imposed shop fronts. In recent years, restoration work has exposed them once again.

The west end of St Peter's Street in November 1954, with East Kent buses partially obscuring views of Holy Cross Church and the Westgate (see page 16). On the left, a Dennis Lancet single decker from 1947 swings away from the small bus station situated just round the corner. On the right, a 1953 Guy Arab IV double decker pulls out of Pound Lane.

A Leyland TD4 outside the East Kent St Stephen's Road Garage in the mid 1950s. The double-decker from 1936 had been rebodied in 1948 by Eastern Counties along with 23 others, a move that considerably lengthened their working life (see page 15). The garage building, also from 1948, was demolished in 1996 to make way for a sheltered residential development.

The new bus station in St George's Lane, during its first week of operation in May 1956. The previous bus station in St Peter's Place (see page 15) closed, not only as it was far too small, but also because the City Council needed the site for the proposed ring road. To persuade East Kent to move, the council offered this larger St George's Lane site in a straight swap.

The Longport coach park in March 1959, with four East Kent AEC Reliance single deckers in evidence. Behind and on the opposite side of Longport, is the Canterbury Technical College (see page 75). The coach park had been created on a site badly effected by the 1942 Blitz (see page 40).

Fallen trees being cleared from a blocked Old Dover Road in the early 1950s. The trees, bordering an empty site on the corner with Nunnery Fields, had been brought down in a heavy storm. The empty site would soon be used for the construction of the new St Mary Bredin church (see page 60).

Firemen demonstrate the use of a turntable ladder during a Fire Station open day in April 1953. This corrugated iron garage building, just off Old Dover Road, was erected in 1943 for the wartime National Fire Service and continued in use until May 1967. A new Fire Station for Canterbury would be opened in Upper Bridge Street during the same month.

Five

The 1960s – Demolition & Modernisation

St George's Crossroads in October 1965, a scene that would shortly be changed completely by the construction of the second stage of the ring road. The building of the ring road's first two stages was one of the major projects in 1960s Canterbury. The first stage had been opened in 1963 (see pages 108 and 109). St George's Roundabout, completed in 1969, would require the demolition of most of the buildings seen here.

The west side of North Lane in the autumn of 1966, with gaps caused by recent demolition. Behind is the bus repair works for East Kent. From the early 1950s onwards, the company acquired individual properties along the North Lane frontage, then demolished them piecemeal. The objective was complete clearance to provide parking spaces for buses visiting the works.

Another section of the west side of North Lane, also from autumn 1966 (see page 12). In the foreground is the surviving part of a fifteenth-century range of timber-framed houses, many of which had disappeared in the early 1950s for bus parking spaces (page 13). The Blue Anchor pub would close in 1971 and become a restaurant.

A busy scene near the North Lane entrance to the West Station Coal Yard in September 1962. The large concrete beams are being transferred from railway wagons to lorries, for transportation to the ring road construction sites. There they will be used in the building of bridges to span the River Stour and railway line.

A more usual view of the Coal Yard, on a wintry day in February 1963 (see page 13). Coal was brought here by rail, then distributed for the domestic market. This was a time before most people had central heating and coal was much in demand, especially on cold days such as this. By the 1980s the sidings had been abandoned. Today the area is covered with houses.

Demolition of old houses in King Street during September 1962. They are typical of the hundreds to be swept away in this decade due to so-called slum clearance. Numbers 48 to 50 King Street are three late seventeenth-century three-storey dwellings, being pulled down for an austere development of flats. Note the demolition worker, top left, peering out from between the jettied gables.

Numbers 10 to 12 King Street, a group dating from the seventeenth and eighteenth centuries, on the corner with Blackfriars Street. It is 1965, only a year from demolition. The late seventeenth-century pair on the right, similar to numbers 48 to 50, are a typical vernacular design of the period, in being brick built on the first two storeys, with timber-framed tiled and jettied gables above.

Above: A brick-built terrace of cottages at numbers 19 to 21 Mill Lane, dating from the second quarter of the nineteenth century. They were built just within the former walled precinct of the Blackfriars. These cottages would disappear in 1966, later to be replaced by a neo-Georgian housing development. This scheme also covered the site of the demolished houses at numbers 10 to 12 King Street.

Right: Firemen tackle a suspicious blaze in an empty house, number 18 Duck Lane, during August 1965. These Edwardian dwellings, by no means slums, were due to come down to clear a path for the proposed third stage of the ring road. The north side of Duck Lane was duly demolished in 1967 and became a temporary-surface car park. The third stage of the ring road was cancelled in 1975.

Prefabricated shops on the Longmarket site, being dismantled prior to the complete redevelopment of the area. The building, encompassing the Longmarket, had been demolished following minor Blitz damage (see page 52). Then in 1947, the prefabs were erected here to house a number of businesses that had been bombed out.

The new Longmarket shortly after completion in August 1961. This development proved too modern for most tastes and its light-weight nature and plain detailing attracted criticism throughout its brief thirty-year life. Nevertheless, the design had its merits, not least of which was that its proportions deliberately allowed generous views of the Cathedral from St George's Street.

Modern Canterbury seen from the Cathedral in February 1968. The 1950s buildings of St George's Street are to the left (see pages 94 and 95). The Longmarket development is in the bottom right-hand corner. To its left, is the 1956 National Provincial Bank, one of the city's best post-war buildings, shamefully demolished this year. Note the vast areas of car parking at this time.

The continental-style roof terrace cafe of the 1960s Longmarket. Beyond the glazed parapet is the rear loading and service area, a less successful part of the scheme because of its poor treatment of the east side of Butchery Lane (see above). This largely unloved version of the Longmarket would be demolished in early 1990 and replaced by an overscale pastiche development.

The top end of Wincheap in 1961, an area that would be transformed by the construction of the ring road. Numbers 1 to 5 Wincheap are on the left (see page 123) and a large Georgian house, now the British Road Service offices, is further right (see page 119). The Georgian house and numbers 1 to 3 Wincheap would perish to make way for Wincheap Roundabout.

Wincheap Green and the top end of Castle Street in May 1961. The triangular building at the junction is The Castle Hotel and Public House. The shops and houses of Wincheap Green are to its right (see page 123). All would vanish in 1963 for the construction of the massive Wincheap Roundabout, which would link the new ring road into the existing road network.

The Man of Kent pub in May 1961, on the junction of Worthgate Place (left) and Pinn Hill, as seen from Wincheap Green. The pub comprises a seventeenth-century house with a Victorian slate-roofed extension. The ring road's first stage would stop short of this point and these buildings would not be affected until the second stage in 1969. Then, the Edwardian houses (right) and Victorian part of the pub would go.

Wincheap Grove in April 1961, with the last of the nineteenth-century terraced houses about to be demolished (see page 31). Wincheap Grove was on the exact line of the ring road, so not only its houses, but also the road itself would soon disappear. The first stage of the ring road opened in 1963 and was named The Rheims Way, after the city twinned with Canterbury.

Numbers 11 to 15 Watling Street, late eighteenth-century houses on the north side of the street, photographed in 1961. The typewriter shop (left) stands on the narrow junction into Rose Lane. Numbers 13 to 15, including the shop, are in the process of demolition, for the City Council's proposed road junction improvement. The remaining houses were safe only for another four years.

The forecourt of Southern Autos' garage in Rose Lane, better known as Marlowe Motors, in about 1962 (see page 91). A veteran Vauxhall from 1909 contrasts with the latest Cresda model. Far right are the rear elevations of the old houses at numbers 7 to 12 Watling Street. They would be demolished in 1965 to provide an extension and office building for Marlowe Motors.

The junction of Watling Street and Rose Lane in 1967 (see opposite). By now, the old houses had gone and Rose Lane (right) had been considerably widened. On the other side of Rose Lane is the overgrown rear garden of the Jacobean house fronting Watling Street. This would later be swallowed up by the buildings of The Marlowe Arcade Development.

The top end of Watling Street with queuing traffic, in early 1969. Further down is the 'new' Congregational Church (see page 73) and further still, the Jacobean house featured in the top picture. On the right, the monstrous multi-storey car park is taking shape. In front, the narrow car parking area will soon become the extension for St George's Lane.

The Little Wonder public house at number 56 Military Road, in 1965. This early nineteenth-century building, possibly with a later front extension, stood on the junction with Notley Street. It had escaped the slum clearance purge of the late 1950s and early 1960s. Therefore, its demolition in 1969 for apparently no reason, is all the more mysterious.

The Saracen's Head public house on the junction of Burgate and Lower Bridge Street. This interesting late seventeenth-century building is a typical example of the period with its tiled and jettied third-storey gables (see page 104). The pub was directly in the path of the ring road's second stage and, despite protestations, was taken down in 1969.

Right: The Duke's Head public house, a post-mediaeval timber-framed building, at number 4 Church Street St Paul's, as seen in 1965. Just visible left, is the brick built workshops for Tice and Company, since demolished. The pub closed in 1975, to become an ever-changing succession of restaurants. The bomb site (right) would become the Magistrates Court car park.

Below: Another Duke's Head public house, at number 62 Wincheap. It is a fairly typical late eighteenth, early nineteenth-century building with a stuccoed front elevation and bay windows, possibly added in the Victorian period. The pub closed in 1972 and is now a private dwelling.

Canterbury citizens of all ages queue outside the Regal Cinema in St George's Place during March 1963, to see *Summer Holiday* starring Cliff Richard and The Shadows (see page 39). The Regal Cinema, built in 1933, had been damaged in the October 1942 raid (during a screening of *Gone With The Wind*), as can be seen by its asymmetrical frontage.

St George's Place and the *Summer Holiday* queue which, by now, has stretched right past Martin Walters garage premises. In the foreground on the right, is a bomb site where once stood an elegant row of late Georgian houses. Just visible right is number 4 St George's Place, a Blitz survivor and the premises for Hastings and Thanet Building Society (see page 38).

St George's Place in May 1960 from the crossroads where New Dover Road and Upper and Lower Chantry Lanes meet (see page 51). Post-war redevelopment has produced the premises for *The Kentish Gazette* and a filling station for Martin Walters. Both have been set well back from the street, in anticipation of St George's Place, later becoming a dual carriageway.

The last prefab awaits demolition on the Churchill Road Estate in February 1967. In the years immediately following the Second World War, a number of small estates containing prefabricated houses, were laid out around the outskirts of Canterbury. The neat 'avenues' of this estate were named after British wartime leaders, such as Montgomery, Harris and of course, Churchill.

Bligh Brothers Ltd, garage and filling station in Dover Street, sometime in the mid 1960s. It was opened in 1960 and had replaced a smaller garage and row of late Georgian cottages on the same site. Dover Street was one of the main routes out of Canterbury in mediaeval times, but is now a quiet back street. Bligh Bros garage complex was later demolished after a very short life.

The Nags Head at 11 Dover Street in 1965, just east of Bligh Bros garage. This was the fourth pub on the site this century. The first, a collection of seventeenth and eighteenth-century buildings on the street frontage, had been replaced by a modern pub, set well back in 1931. Nags Head mark two was Blitzed and later replaced by a pub in a prefab. The Nags Head seen here, opened in March 1958.

Further east still, we find this charming row of seventeenth-century cottages at 13 to 16 Dover Street, known locally as Holman Cottages. This picture dates from May 1960, after their eleventh hour salvation from the bulldozer. Adjacent at the far end of the row is an eighteenth-century shop, once run by Holman Brothers, but now a hairdresser. The Nag's Head pub sign is just visible, right.

An interesting group of buildings on Dover Street's north side, in November 1962. Far right, an extension to Martin Walters Garage had replaced an oast house in 1960. At this time, the three timber-framed properties (numbers 50 to 52) were threatened with demolition. In the event, the two late-mediaeval cottages perished in 1964 but the former Beehive pub (nearest the camera) was saved.

Left: The battered frontage of the Freemason's Tavern in St Margaret's Street, just before demolition in 1965 (see page 96). Canterbury's post-war road plans included not only a ring road, but also a relief road straight through the centre of the city. The Freemason's Tavern was in its path. Just beyond the pub is the frontage to the Marlowe Theatre (see page 124).

Below: Hawk's Lane, just off St Margaret's Street in November 1966, when its future as a lane was under threat by the relief road. The buildings on its south side (left) were safe, but would face directly onto the proposed dual carriageway. Everything on the north side was to go. Much advance demolition along the route had already taken place before the plans were eventually dropped.

Six

In More Recent Years

Taken from Telephone House, this cityscape shows an area that has undergone many changes since being photographed in 1935 (see page 9). Centre, is the British Road Service office building, constructed shortly after their previous office was demolished for the ring road (see page 108). The whole depot, now empty, would give way to a new Habitat store.

The bottom end of Union Street from Union Place in 1988. On the left, the early nineteenth-century King William IV pub was the only building in the street to survive the 1960s slum clearance. Now it was to avoid another round of demolition. The Toyota Showrooms and Royal Mail Sorting Office behind, would soon be pulled down and later, the site redeveloped for student accommodation.

The King William IV in 1988, this time taken from Victoria Row. More of the Sorting Office complex and entrance gates to the depot yard are in the foreground. After demolition in 1989, a large archaeological investigation uncovered the extensive remains of St Gregory's Priory. The Priory had been founded in the 1080s and the last remains above ground were demolished in 1848.

Numbers 13 and 14 Northgate, early nineteenth-century houses, in January 1983. In the mid 1960s, many such dwellings in Northgate had been demolished, ostensibly for road widening. This pair survived as they were slightly set back from the street. Then, when the electricity works site (behind) was cleared, they still hung on. Sadly, the pair finally perished in 1988.

Early nineteenth-century cottages in Sturry Road, under threat in 1987. I photographed them just after they had been acquired by Invicta Motors, who wanted the site to extend their Commercial Vehicles Centre. The cottages duly came down months later, prior to the complete redevelopment and expansion of the Invicta site.

The west side of Stour Street in April 1987, following the demolition of the former Towers Meat Store. When this apparently Victorian building was pulled down, a much older timber frame was discovered beneath the brick facades. The rendered houses at numbers 30 to 34, date from the 1880s and had replaced a row of ancient timbered dwellings, of which a water colour exists.

This bleak site was once Canterbury Gas Works, that had been closed and demolished at the end of the 1960s (see page 30). When photographed in September 1977, the vast brick and concrete foundations had been exposed by the Canterbury Archaeological Trust, who had been working on the site for two years. Much Roman material was discovered.

Numbers 10 to 16 Wincheap in November 1974. As numbers 4 to 7 prior to renumbering, they narrowly escaped demolition when Wincheap Roundabout was constructed. By 1980, they were extremely ruinous and were once more threatened with demolition. Fortunately, after being awarded a conservation grant, they were comprehensively restored in 1981.

Another nearby derelict house, number 11 Worthgate Place. For many years it had been hidden behind the buildings of Wincheap Green, but made its presence known following demolitions for the ring road (see page 108). The house, which abuts the city wall behind, is now restored and has recently been painted shocking pink!

Left: The impressive front of The Marlowe Theatre in December 1980, shortly after its closure had been announced. Built in 1927, it cleverly imitates a sixteenth-century vernacular design. Left, is the Marlowe car park, extended in size following the demolition of the Freemason's Tavern in 1965 (see page 118). On the right is Slatters Hotel, an early 1960s building.

Below: The rear of the Marlowe Theatre from the multi-storey car park in about 1981. Nearest the camera is the stage end extension building, designed by City Architect Hugh Wilson and built in 1951. Surrounding it is the Marlowe car park which, together with the site of the theatre, would shortly be completely redeveloped.

Right: The Canterbury Archaeological Trust excavating part of the Marlowe car park adjacent to Rose Lane, in advance of the proposed redevelopment. The west ends of two different St Mary Bredin churches have been uncovered. To the right, a trust member sits on the west wall of the mediaeval church, demolished in the early 1870s. The substantial brick foundations for its Victorian replacement are on the left (see page 60).

Below: June 1982 and demolition of the theatre is well underway. Ripped out theatre seats provide a convenient vantage point from which one Canterbury citizen watches the theatre's final scene. The crane tears into the 1927 auditorium, whilst the 1951 extension (left) awaits a similar fate. Following demolition and more archaeological excavation, work started on the Marlowe Arcade Development.

Left: The empty butcher's shop of Brickies of Kent at 18 Lower Bridge Street, in September 1974. By this time, it was hemmed in on both sides by large modern buildings. Right is the Inland Revenue Building (1972) and left, the premises for Invicta Motors, completed in 1963 (see page 86). Later, Invicta's purchased and demolished Brickies for an office extension.

Below: The Dover Street end of Martin Walter's garage in February 1989. Mediaeval cottages that abutted the garage had been demolished in 1964 (see page 117). The garage itself had replaced an oast house in 1960, when the cottages still stood abutted to it. Therefore, the gable-shaped side wall actually survives from the oast. Note the re-used Caen stone. The garage and old wall went in 1995.

Right: Numbers 165 and 167 Old Dover Road under demolition in May 1984. These late nineteenth-century houses, long since divided into flats, gave way to a new block of flats. As has clearly been demonstrated in this section, the destruction of old buildings did not entirely cease following the official recognition of the importance of conservation in the early 1970s.

Below: The empty premises for Caffyns Ltd, on the corner of New Dover Road and Upper Chantry Lane in June 1984. The garage, encompassing filling station, showrooms and service area, was put up for Maltby's Ltd (see page 24). Later, Caffyns took over and, in 1951, built a rear extension in the same style. The garage would soon be demolished and replaced by a furniture store.

The Holy Cross and St Peter's Primary School in February 1971. It was built at around the turn of the twentieth century, a time when the top end of St Peter's Place led straight into open countryside. In 1963, St Peter's Place became part of the ring road and a less attractive place to have a school. The building has since been demolished and replaced by flats.

St Dunstan's Primary School in London Road, my old school, pictured in May 1974 sometime after its closure. This Victorian school once had separate blocks for boys, girls and infants. The original boy's block can be seen on the left. The empty site was once occupied by prefabricated classrooms and the playground. The surviving parts would later be converted for residential use.